The Unruly Monkey

The UNRULY MONKEY

REFLECTIONS ON LIFE, LOVE, AND MONEY

John Train

ARTISAN PRESS

TABLE OF CONTENTS

The mind is an unruly monkey.

WANG MING (VI CENTURY)

FOREWORD

Here are a few lessons of my life, sometimes learned the hard way. They were not assembled as a philosophy, but are random thoughts as they occurred over time to this particular "unruly monkey,"* sorted by categories.

While all for virtue, I have tried to hold back on moralizing, and on rephrasing the familiar. (On the other hand, many things that have been said but forgotten deserve to be said again.)

To "vary the line," as one says in painting, I have added little stories here and there, and a handful of practical notions.

Think of it like a cookbook: Instead of reading continuously, wait for an interesting idea and stop a while.

J.T.

---

*Montaigne called it a wild horse, perhaps invoking its propensity to rush about in herds, like Ionesco's rhinoceroses.

HUMAN NATURE

Everything Human Is Cyclical

An idea that was once popular will again be popular, in art, styles of government, fashions in clothing. . . .

Pathe Mathos — "Learn Through Suffering"

The great teachers are *suffering* and *time*.

Foolish acts bring painful experiences. Painful experiences bring wisdom.

Defeat is a stimulus; victory breeds complacency: catastrophic.

A fool can't accept good advice.

People Try To Appear What They Fear They Are Not

Then they become it.

Elsa Maxwell, from the wrong side of the tracks, emerges as a social arbiter; Teddy Roosevelt and Ernest Hemingway, fragile as boys, remake themselves as bruisers. The great investors in my "Money Masters" books came from impoverished families. Ambition, creative genius, a will to power, and a craving for wealth often flow from a feeling of inferiority in youth. But in time that feeling, like the tannin in a good claret, should work itself off. Otherwise the residue sours the personality.

How others react to our behavior will often reveal our real as distinct from ostensible motivation.

Freedom

Obsession with freedom leads a democracy to breakdown, as described in the eighth book of Plato's *Republic*, just as did a craving for excessive wealth during the oligopoly phase.

Three Kinds of Swede

The three categories, all found in the films of Ingmar Bergman, are: first, the prickly and extremely punctual upper class,* who arrive within a minute of the appointed time for an appointment (which Swedes occasionally set in the *door* of a restaurant). Second, the gloomy intellectual couple who conduct inquests on their marriage, hour after hour, year after year; and third, the boisterous citizen who resembles certain Norwegians or Americans.

Clothes Are a Message

Being pleasantly turned out shows respect to others and for yourself.**

The folks who spend the weekend in town wearing country tweeds are intimating that only by accident are they not off tramping over their estates. The banker turned out conservatively except for a jazzy tie is playing a counterpoint to a theme: "I'm reliable, but also a free spirit." Some of the prominent Carter and Clinton administration staffers took to propping their heavy work boots on their White House desks: "I'm still a plain good old

---

*My Stockholm in-laws would sometimes silently circle in the street before the house where they were invited for dinner. The dean of guests, having determined his rank through sidelong glances, would touch the doorbell at 7:29.59. The door would fly open and the hostess, standing right behind the parlor maid, would greet the arrivals. Only once safely inside would the guests talk to each other.

**Some highly personal observations for men: Let clothes be comfortably loose, appropriate, and well cut. Avoid a plaster of Paris fit. Replace your coat hangers with others that have corrugated tops on the crossbars, so trousers don't slip off, and with substantial shoulders. Have flaps with buttons on your inside jacket pockets to foil pickpockets and avoid having things drop out.

boy," they were saying, "not like you city dudes." Perhaps. Billionaire Anglophile haberdasher Ralph Lauren appears in Moscow dressed in tattered ranching duds, staying in the U.S. embassy.

Ritual

Ceremonies, by tying us to our past, tell us that we are important, and strengthen us in hard times.

Misplaced Confidence

Almost all drivers think they possess superior driving skill.***

All executives rate themselves in the top quartile as to ability to get along with others, and 25% of them put themselves in the top 1%. 70% put themselves in the top quartile as to leadership. In calculating odds and in making investment predictions, the situation is similar. If 80% of the analyst community likes a stock, they are wrong 60% of the time. If investors are unanimous that a stock must rise, it must decline.

Trumpery

"I have observed," pronounced Nick the Greek, the most eminent betting odds-maker of his day, "that newspaper publicity is usually followed by a jail sentence." In England, and Europe generally, talking about your ancestors, important connections, and other boastfulness**** tolerated in a growing country are deplored.

Rubber soles, or thin rubber half-soles over your leather soles, keep the feet dry and warm. As one man speaking to women, I note that modesty and functionality appeal to me more than self-conscious elaboration. The confections on the fashion catwalks often seem demented.

***See "The Psychology of Decision Making" by Amos Tversky, in *Behavioral Finance and Decision Theory in Investment Management*.

*****Le nom d'un fou se trouve partout*, say the French: "A nitwit's name is seen everywhere," e.g., Donald Trump.

Bien Dans Sa Peau

Rightly do the French describe a person with a harmonious character as "comfortable in his skin." Often, he also puts others at their ease.

Gravitas

I like the Roman expression, "A free man walks slowly."

Do not sneer, or exploit another's adversity.

Troubled People

They repeat destructive patterns. By changing the scenery, troubled people hope to flee their shadow . . . in vain.

Troubled people will trouble you.

Moralistic indignation bespeaks inner rage.

Be suspicious of people who are very suspicious.

Do not argue with a neurosis. Cut the knot and depart.*

Few people are as sour as a disappointed romantic.

The Overpowering Parent Syndrome

I am occasionally drawn to multifaceted intelligent charming people who are habitually late. Sometimes they had a parent who was too good to be true, an impossible act to follow. So by making people wait, my friends are taking a little delayed revenge on that overwhelming figure.

ૐ

If Survival Is the First Law, the Second, Perforce, Is Taking Advantage of Others

ૐ

---

*Laura Riding, troubled poetess, having churned up Robert Graves into an emotional lather, convinced him to join her in a suicide pact. Leaping from a window in St. Peter's Square, Hammersmith, she crumpled to the stones, horribly injured. Prudently, he descended part way before following suit, and was unharmed.

We Have Concentric Ethical Systems

First, inside the family. Then, friends, whom we treat and who treat us correctly; and then outsiders. So in a business relationship with a distant group, stay closely on top of things, or expect trouble.

When Old Lovers Meet Long After

Six people are present: the two regarding each other now, two sets of youthful images in their minds' eyes, and two memories of former passion.

Gods As Metaphor

The Greek deities sometimes represent hormones. The irresistible power of Cupid's bow is the rush of the "falling in love" hormone, testosterone,* Mars is adrenaline plus testosterone, panic fear (inspired by Pan) is aroused by glucocorticoids, Venus is norepinephrine plus dopamine, while long-term attachment, the glue of families, is linked to vasopressin and oxytocin.

Work

Your work is whatever you do in the middle of the day: for a lawyer, papers; for a society hostess, arranging occasions; and for a prisoner, making license plates. *Desirable* work should be fulfilling, useful to society, and suitably compensated, whether in cash, love, or honor.

❧

Indolence invites decay: A yacht is happier in a wind than in the doldrums, when things shake apart. "Work is love made manifest," said Khalil Gibran.

❧

To be happy in your work: what joy! (My family motto is AMOR HONOR LABOR.)

---

*Odd to think of Cupid as an icon for $C_{19}H_{28}O_2$! The amorous coupling of Mars and Venus signifies love calming aggression, or, as they say, "Make love, not war." Alas, men are built to fight, and women love warriors. The Cupid—or lust—hormone must be faster-acting than the Venus hormone because the brain circuitry of Don Juans (and animals) must be fired in a hurry.

Crazy Fallacies Intoxicate Fanatics

. . . not obvious truths. We yearn to believe, and some people will die rather than change their mindset.* Pluralistic creeds, such as Hinduism or democracy, can welcome a new deity or a new idea, while a jealous god, including a Stalin or a Pol Pot, wants his opponents dead.

Praxis

The legislator should know the world and have worked in government,** the art critic should have painted, the military staff officer must serve in the field, the philosopher should understand business (which is what most people actually do), and the architect should spend time in construction. When an intellectual holds forth on economic policy, see if he knows the profit margin of a supermarket.

Futurology

The ups and downs in our view of the future, including market cycles—from terror to euphoria and points between—derive from swings in crowd psychology, not objective reality.

When You Are Angry, Stop Everything

And don't engage in tit-for-tat ripostes. Listen! then summarize the opponent's arguments until he sees that you fully understand him.

---

*Cooper's Creek describes English explorers in the Australian outback who do not know the plants and insects that would nourish them. They see the aborigines subsisting in the same habitat, but will not deign to ask for help. All but one die. He, free from the inhibitions of his defunct companions, appeals to the aborigines, who save him.

**Thus, governors, who have struggled to deal with reality, usually make better presidents than senators, who manipulate ideas.

As Sharks Have Feeding Frenzies, Humans Have Killing Frenzies

The German word is *Mörderlust*. When Stalin assigned a quota of liquidations — 20,000 let us say — to Khruschev, Nikita K. would often boost the take to 30,000, to show his zeal.

Lead Not into Temptation

Alas, many of us are dishonest if not watched.

Two's Company

A third, by playing social politics, affects the dynamic.

The Need to Babble Bears No Relation to the Message Itself

Noisy people have little to say.*

❧

The brilliant question is often the one nobody dares ask.

❧

People have different personalities in different languages.

❧

The boss tells the funniest jokes.

If Variety Is the Spice of Life, A Pinch of Malice Is the Pepper of Gossip

But shun tale-bearing.

---

*I like the "optical" conversation: "Hey, Chuck! Great to see ya!" "Great to see ya, Jimbo!" "Chuck, you're looking great!" "Yeah, you too!" "Ya seen Jack?" "Yeah, He looked good!" "Well, nice to see ya!" "Great seein' ya!"

We Drown In Facts

Too many facts crowd out wisdom. A glance may reveal more than a microscope.

❧

Know thyself, of course—but particularly how little one can ever really know.

❧

Say "I don't know" frequently.

Perspective

As the artist steps back from the canvas to view his painting, we, too, should contemplate what we are becoming. More than pursuing specific objectives, such as becoming a success, one should consider one's character and what *kind* of person one wants to be.

HAPPINESS

The Pursuit of Happiness

Happiness is not to be pursued directly, like pleasure. It flows from self-realization.

❧

The greatest blessing in life is a cheerful disposition. After that, closely linked, comes good health.

❧

We crave a mate, a prince, a god, a purpose: something outside ourselves. Most tiresome is a life turned inward, whose thermometer is the frequency of "I" in conversation.

❧

Concern for others is indispensable to happiness.

❧

You adjust to unexpected good fortune after six months or so.

❧

Most people think that the right amount of money is 40% more than they have.

Bad Advice

"If at first you don't succeed, try, try again." No! First, correct your original mistake.

❧

"You can't be too rich or too thin." (On the contrary!)

❧

"If you have it, flaunt it." (A far better maxim is, "live quietly.")

Costly Display

The rich tell each other about their costly indulgences for reassurance, like patients sharing symptoms. (Happiness is more likely to flow from a generally austere habit of life.)

Now, Here

A walk is not "muscle toning." Dinner is not "networking." Parents and children being affectionate with each other are not spending "quality time." Reading for delight is not a "learning experience." Taking photographs is not the purpose of travel. Let the joy of each moment be its sufficient purpose, then and there.

In the Accidents of Travel Lie Its Charm

And it is through life's setbacks that we grow. Do not fear difficult tests.

Life

Cleanliness, once next to godliness, has now replaced it. Underneath it all, though, life is a great messy goulash.

Elements of Contentment

A dear companion, loyal children and friends*, a community, a lovable country, a cozy home, a vocation, a traditional culture, a little too much money, not quite enough time, and perhaps a slight sense of danger.

Pericles:

"The secret of happiness is freedom, and the secret of freedom is a brave heart."

---

*Confucius: "A friend coming from far away. What a pleasure!"

YOUNG AND OLD

Yardsticks

In youth, you measure age from when you started. When old, you measure back from the far end.

Dedication

The immature yearn for dramatic causes, usually harmful.

Talk or Example

Children are less influenced by your preaching than your deeds, and your comments about others. So before children, praise excellence.

Advice to the Young

Aim high!

ॐ

Some people are idea-manipulators, whether of numbers or words; some are thing-manipulators, whether manufacturers or farmers; and some are people-manipulators, who govern or manage. You tend to drift into the occupation that is usual where you grow up: Thus, New Yorkers are idea-manipulators, and are comfortable as lawyers, financiers and advertisers; Washingtonians enter government; in Cleveland you manufacture; and so on. But some of us are born in the wrong place. How, then, do you discover your true bent? By experimenting. So let a young person try several trades to see what fits, or take the remarkable Johnson O'Connor Foundation aptitude tests, which match up your strengths with possible occupations.

And to the Old

Aging well is a high art.

ॐ

Consciously lengthen your walking stride and swing your arms and shoulders when you get older.

ॐ

Keep the mind active solving problems and learning.

ॐ

Nourish your affections.

Young and Old

Older people are much more likely (50%) to be "very happy" than young people (about 30%).* In youth, we see others as a body with a spirit. In age, we think of ourselves as a spirit with a body.

An elderly person thinks of himself as a continuum, extending from the sandbox through vigorous youth and middle age to fading. The observer sees only the wrinkled present. The differences between young and old flow in part from the role of the young as creators and the old as conservators. A young person brushes aside the inconveniences of life like a general in the field or a painter in his one-room studio. (Similarly, a young, growing company never has enough cash to finance its expansion, and always suffers from an out-of-date organization.) The older person, having created whatever fortune he is going to have, becomes preoccupied with amenities.

Toys

One learns eventually which childhood possessions can be abandoned: dolls, marbles, posters, little-used gadgets, collections of knives. Later you decide you don't need to collect acquaintances for the sake of fattening your

---

American Sociological Review (April, 2008), reporting on a thirty-year annual survey of 1500 to 3000 men and women.

address book, or vast amounts of information (including much political information); or constant activity; or the admiration of persons whom one does not admire oneself; and above all, excess property.

Evening

Beware an old man's follies — financial or sentimental.

The Hook

Distressing though it is for individuals, the interest of creation demands death and new birth. The director of the great variety show, bored by our antics, hauls us offstage.

⁂

The world existed for countless ages before we appeared. Since we are not troubled by what we missed then, let us be tranquil about missing the unknowable future, which anyway ends when the earth is overwhelmed by the sun.

Living

The songs we have sung, the dreams we have dreamt and the loves we have lived are ours always.

Vale

Like sparks, we fly into the night.

MANAGEMENT

Distrust Management Fads

"Management by exception," "systems engineering," "critical path," "PERT," "built to last," "excellence," "six sigma," *Mitbestimmung* (labor-management collaboration in decision-making), computer-generated solutions. And of course spare us from the "management secrets" of Genghis Khan, Attila the Hun, Sun Tsu, or whoever. Nothing equals highly competent, experienced managers talking to each other. The Navy used PERT as much for its effect on Congress and the public as for management, as it freed Admiral Raborn and his able staff from interference: "They could point to the 'system' as a guarantor of good performance. The Critical Path method devised in the DuPont Company (was) never allowed to interfere with DuPont's effective managers." (Prof. Frank Davidson, M.I.T.). Peter Drucker, a wonderful management consultant, wrote that Rapell Ackolf saved him "as he had saved countless others from descending into mindless model building — the disease that all but destroyed so many of the business schools."

Do Not Instantly Grant A Request

Consider it a while.

Seed a New Organization with First-Class People

Only they will hire other first-class people. An organization should be lean, except at the start of a project, when things should be comfortably staffed and carefully engineered, to avoid another Leaning Tower of Pisa.

"Esquire"

As the practice of law declines from a high calling to a rapacious business, American (not English) lawyers style themselves "esquire," claiming the chivalry they have forsaken.

Talk Out Problems Face to Face

Never exchange angry memoranda.

ॐ

Let the person who is bothered talk first.

ॐ

Avoid long arguments with a quarrelsome boor: Leave.*

Devolution

The boss should reject descriptions of problems ending with, "What do you think?" To make the sender think, route them back with an arrow at the query and a circle around the word *You.*

ॐ

Too Many Pressures on an Organism and It Crumbles; Too Few, and It Becomes Soft

ॐ

Courtesy

Speak and write clearly, as an act of courtesy (and effectiveness).

ॐ

Good manners are extremely persuasive.**

---

*Consider the maxim, "Do not argue with inferiors."

**Colonel House, President Wilson's advisor, manifested exquisite courtesy. Responding to my father's flattering comment, he observed that when he was young in Texas, men usually carried revolvers. If a squabble became violent, you could be in real trouble. So he learned to be polite, very polite indeed.

The Leader

An organization without a leader is a family without a parent. A great leader is worth a hundred mediocrities.

ᚹ

A leader has a vision and conveys it.

ᚹ

He is formidable, admirable, and surprising.

ᚹ

He is a master of whatever the organization does, but needs business skill more than technical skill.

ᚹ

A leader who bases policies on polls or meetings is merely a follower. Wellington did not hold councils of war.

ᚹ

A leader will be ruined if he welcomes optimistic flattery more than cool objectivity.

ᚹ

To engender loyalty, be loyal to those you lead; be willing to give up a lot for them.

ᚹ

A good leader decides the large questions and delegates the others, except for details that set the tone of the organization.

ᚹ

A good leader sees and is seen on regular walkabouts.* He talks to people, understands their concerns, and hears their suggestions. He is noticed picking things up and straightening rugs and pictures.

Look Serious When Giving Orders

General George Patton said he would cashier any officer who issued commands with a smile. He practiced what he called his "war face." Eisenhower smiled mostly for photographers.

Fair Warning

When Admiral Crowe succeeded General Vessey as Chairman of the Joint Chiefs of Staff, Vessey said to him, "This (the Pentagon) is a very large organization. If you think of *the worst thing that could possibly happen*, it's happening somewhere here right now."

"Surtout pas Trop de Zèle"

This curious rule of Talleyrand's for his Foreign Ministry subordinates, "Don't buzz about,"** or don't be in a hurry, resembles Churchill's instructions to his ambassador in Washington during the time of Nazi victories: "Let your manner be bland and phlegmatic." Churchill liked to repeat the importance of calm.

---

*The story goes that talking to his soldiers, Frederick the Great often asked:

> "What is your name?"
> "How old are you?"
> "Are your food and quarters all right?"

> The troops were told to respond:
> "Schultz (or whatever), Your Majesty."
> "Nineteen, Your Majesty."
> "Both, Your Majesty."

> One day the great man varied his routine, asking:
> "How old are you?"
> "Schultz, Your Majesty."
> "What is your name?"
> "Nineteen, Your Majesty."

> "Either you're crazy or I am!"
> "Both, Your Majesty."

**Another interpretation could be to avoid doctrinaire enthusiasm. Talleyrand, while indolent and corrupt, sought what was best for his country and the peace of Europe, not for his current ruler. Another of his remarkable expressions was *"Il faut jamais être pauvre diable"* — "Never become pitiful." (Once you've been humiliated, it's hard to regain respect. People sympathize, then give advice, then stay away. A wounded animal — or state — will be attacked.) A fascinating conversationalist, Talleyrand avoided talking about himself, the "moi-je" monologue of the bore.

If Something Is Not Worth Doing at All, It's Not Worth Doing Well

❦

Family Loyalty Competes with Corporate Fidelity

Thus, America has weak families but wonderful companies. Cultures with close-knit families often produce unreliable employees. "If I don't steal from the (state-owned) company, I'm stealing from my family."

Since Flattery is Self-Interested, Receive It with a Touch of Irony

To gratify a visiting author, do not prominently display one of his books on a coffee table; Let it peek slyly from a shelf.

❦

Praise people for qualities that they *hope* to acquire.

❦

At the End of Every Meeting, Fix the Time of the Next One and Assign Tasks to Specific Individuals

❦

Begin Meetings Exactly on Time

❦

Date All Papers

. . . particularly successive drafts.

STATECRAFT

Hostile Governments May Not Be Diabolical, Just Confused

Still, when Caesar approaches the Rubicon, do not assume that he is on a fishing trip. Prepare for the worst.

Scandals

Is a public man's sleazy private life entirely his own, to be passed over by journalists? Perhaps if he can't manage his own life, he cannot manage ours.

Political Ambassadors

Naming politically connected incompetents as ambassadors insults both the host country and its official community, and degrades the career. Let us instead create an order like the O.B.E. or the *Légion d'Honneur*—e.g., the "Order of the Republic"—for which the ambitious can intrigue without weakening our foreign relations.*

❦

In Great Affairs, Personal Ties Are Central

❦

Economic Sanctions Are Like Rain Dances

They give us something to do. Alas, they don't work: one leak sinks the canoe. And they enrich smugglers and gangsters.

---

* Ambassador Mac Toon was visiting an admiral commanding a battle group in the Mediterranean on board his aircraft carrier. Toward the end of the visit, the admiral asked, "What's it like being an ambassador? I've always thought that when I retire I might want to try it." Toon replied, "That's funny. I've always thought that after I retire I might try my hand commanding a battle group."

Train's First Law: Price Controls Increase Prices

. . . by inhibiting production. Higher prices stimulate production, thus lowering prices. Thanks to rent control, for years New York only built a fraction of the rental apartments that one would expect in a city of its demographics. Thanks to controls, Argentina actually has meat shortages.

Train's Second Law:
The More the Government Does Something, the Less There Is of It

The government costs about twice as much and takes about three times as long as the private sector to do any given thing. In New York, parochial schools deliver a much better education than the public school system at a fraction of the cost per pupil. At the limit, under Communism the government does almost everything, and people receive very little indeed. "We pretend to work and they pretend to pay us," said Soviet workers. The Bulgarian variation was, "they can't pay us as little as we work."

Professor C. Northcote Parkinson gave me this example: "Ronald Reagan, when he was governor of California, asked me to address his cabinet. I told him about the Bay Bridge, which connects San Francisco with Oakland. Fourteen painters were appointed to paint the bridge from one end to the other, and then paint their way back again. Since then the spraying machine has been introduced, so that the job can be done much faster.

"Nevertheless, by the time Ronald Reagan had become governor, the number of men engaged in permanently painting the bridge had risen, I believe, to 77! After my talk to his cabinet Ronald Reagan tackled this problem, and was able, I heard, to cut the staff of painters to 50-odd. I don't doubt that they have since crept back up to 90."

Makework Programs Reduce Employment

Their cost consumes the productive investment that creates real jobs.

The Institutions of a Decaying Society Work in Reverse

The criminal justice system breeds crime, schools develop irresponsibility, welfare encourages dependency. Still, humanity has a tremendous instinct for self-preservation. Eventually come reform and renewal.

❧

Untended, a garden runs to weeds, and an old tree decays and sprouts fungi. *Social* decay breeds such parasites as drugs and crime. So just as gardens need tending, we must teach young people civic responsibility.

Great Ages

Sometimes a country catches fire, and like a shooting star streaks across the dark sky of history. As Hegel says, "its clock strikes." Then it flames out, and sinks again into the dreaming sleep of centuries. Thus, the Mongols, Macedon, Rome, the Viking-Normans, the Ottomans, Spain, Portugal, England. . . .

Demagogues

Most people cannot determine the truth of large questions. So any authoritative demagogue who presents vehement arguments that appeal to interest and emotion will gain a following. A politician must be *for* something, and thus against its opposite, which his followers demonize.

Political opinions do not derive from a clear view of the future, but the advantage of one's faction.

Power-seekers—not only bureaucrats but also demagogues, politicized intellectuals, and foundation executives—see themselves as levers of change.* They view civil society, notably the market economy, which performs this function better, as a rival.

---

*The social activist's creed: "We're all on earth to help others. What the others are here for, we don't know." (W. H. Auden)

History Can be Read as the Eternal Struggle between King John and the Barons

Either, ruling alone, is intolerable. The barons will oppress the people, who cry to the King for relief. But unchecked, King John becomes a dictator. Modern barons—unions, ethnic pressure groups, manufacturers, and the rest—struggle for monopoly power, until King John—the government—intervenes to break it up again.

Civil Society

A child here receives constant practice in parliamentary procedure: electing class committees, team captains and the like, and learning to accept their decisions; European children receive little or none.

Every American village has a rich network of mediating organizations, including churches, hospitals, museums, schools, community funds, the Masons, Elks, Lions, and other such organizations, a bar association, charitable foundations and the rest. A big city may have thousands.* Most of American society outside large cities is so solidly based on these organizations that it could probably manage without Washington at all.

Five Necessary Qualities of a President

The President must understand foreign affairs and military matters. A mistaken policy can lead to war. (President Eisenhower, in periods of great stress, knew when to be firm and when to yield. President Kennedy, inexperienced, but aspiring to being a "magnificent lion," ran grave risks, and embroiled the country in a failed land war in Asia and a failed invasion of Cuba.)

꒳

---

*One count found three hundred Italian-American organizations in and around New York. Such groups should be called Civil Society Organizations (C.S.O.) rather than Non-Governmental Organizations (N.G.O.), a term that implies that government should ordinarily do everything.

Political skill. Otherwise, congress runs the presidency. Lyndon Johnson could manipulate anybody.

⁊⋲

Administrative skill, without which the job is overwhelming. The President must delegate trifles.

⁊⋲

Understanding business, which is what people actually do. Kennedy and Mitterand wrecked business confidence, producing sharp recessions.

⁊⋲

The chief of state should appear virtuous.

The Bully Pulpit

Fortunate are the countries with modest, serious constitutional monarchs, such as Spain or Sweden, or virtuous presidents, such as Washington, who provide a model and guide.*

Savonarola

The perfectibility of humanity is a fearsome heresy, particularly in a leader who will be corrupted by power. As his paranoia deepens, real and fancied opponents multiply, who must be sacrificed on the altar of social order.

The Cycle of Government

Plato was right: Each style of government is undone by the exaggeration of its own *idée de base*, just as too much of a stimulant becomes a poison. Thus, hereditary rule by descendants of the able decays, yielding to oligopoly rule by powerful magnates. Their ostentation in turn provokes the envious commonality to overthrow them and take power through populism, whose cry is "freedom!" But an excess of freedom leads to chaos. That, in turn, invites a Bonaparte to fill the vacuum. Bonaparte makes himself hereditary, creating

---

*Our kings and queens — the rock singers and movie stars who fill the pages of trashy magazines — drip slime into the heart of national life.

a monarchy, and eventually a theocracy—a Mao or Stalin, whose word is law. When the theocrat's pretensions become intolerable, the military assume power, in due course to be displaced by leading civilians—aristocracy, rule by the able. Thus the cycle continues.

Each stage has its conceptual framework. Aristocrats revere tradition, virtue and excellence; plutocrats worship Mammon and economic development; democracy loves youth and the common touch (a grin calling itself Jimmy or Bill) and new ideas masquerading as "science." The theocrat, a bearded elder, bases his claims on received wisdom, and deprecates novelty.

The Essential Virtue of Law Is Impartial Predictability, Not the Latest Idea of Justice

One's conception of justice is a political judgment. You learn a dozen completely different philosophies in law school.

ॐ

The Serious Voter Should Understand Business, Politics, and War

ॐ

Demography Is Destiny

"Anatomy is destiny," said Freud, but so too is demography. A huge population influx, such as Europeans and then Africans into the Americas, or the barbarians into the Roman Empire, or, perhaps, Muslims into Europe, scrambles society.

Likewise geography, "the eye of history," according to Ortelius. Britain and Japan both recognize that they are America's outposts, and can probably rely on the American defense umbrella. Both were civilized from the mainland: Japan by the reception of Buddhism under Prince Shotoku, and England first by the Romans and then by Christianity. Both have often gone to war to prevent the main continental power from dominating the military jumping-off points: For Britain, the low countries, for Japan, Korea. Is it a coincidence that these ancient islands are still constitutional monarchies?

In any event, for an individual, *character* is destiny.

Égalité

The French Revolution's cry of *Liberté Égalité Fraternité* is demonstrably absurd. "Be my brother or die!" Equality implies eliminating everybody important: far from fraternal! Liberty and equality are contradictory, since only heavy government control—meaning reduced liberty—can prevent the able and energetic from rising to the top and staying there.

⁊⁊

Equality is an important legal conception, not a fact of anthropology. And without respect for proper hierarchy, systems break down.

⁊⁊

Religion consoles us for inequality. As religion fades, the cry for equality grows louder.

⁊⁊

Having overturned the tyrant, the revolutionary seizes his throne.

⁊⁊

In a "people's republic," the perfection of equality, a great figure's disfavor can still be worth a common citizen's life.

Uneven Distribution

One reason for capital inequality is that after a lifetime of work and saving, older people own more than do young people starting out. And an influx of poor immigrants lowers the average income temporarily. However, a rich person may not use up more than a poor person. He does not eat more; rather, he may just manage more assets as a curator. It is better that entrepreneurs and well-rewarded executives should run enterprises, rather than dim bureaucrats. As a modest shareholder of Microsoft, I am undismayed that Mr. Gates, who created the company, owns vastly more of it and has been compensated magnificently.

Inflation Reflects Social Morale

One can gauge a country's inflation rate by the density of the graffiti seen on the trip in from the airport, or the debris in the streets. Very few scribbles = a virtuous society = low inflation. Another index is clothing: high times seem to invite both daring clothing and inflation.

After the bubble bursts, people dress conservatively and inflation is tamed.

ॐ

The Mass Can Be Persuaded To Commit Any Crime

ॐ

Countries Are Saved By a Handful of Heroes

ॐ

Disinformation

Political warfare is the most cost-effective form of competition between states, and within political warfare, disinformation. In their heyday, the Soviets were at any time operating a thousand-odd *dezinformatsia* campaigns in the West. The Nazis made a similar effort. So did the British, operating near the top of American society and government, desperate to draw the US into World War II.

The Good Spy

Contra James Bond, the good spy is a little gray man with his cover on his back who has trouble catching the eye of a headwaiter. "A shabby exterior but a will of iron," says Sun Tzu.

ॐ

A Government Easily Seduces Intellectuals through Small Recognitions

ॐ

Compliance

Prime Minister Thatcher ordered Robin Butler (later Lord B.) to dispose of that bicycle he was pedaling around Whitehall: undignified, possibly dangerous. He abandoned it in the entrance of the Cabinet Office, where, rusting, it was shown to me years later. Then he got hold of a different one and pedaled around on it instead.

Conflict

When deep demographic or ideological changes shift and grind against each other, they produce disturbances on the surface called wars. A few things are worse than war, notably national dishonor, which may just postpone the war.

How Institutions Decay

The initial stage of an institution is dedicated to the founder's high purpose. In the second, it pursues its own advancement. In the third, its functionaries seek personal gain.

Bureaucracy

Authority yearns to cast off restraint.

❧

In dangerous times, government claims dangerous powers.

❧

Bureaucrats exist to regulate. Big business can cope with over-regulation; less so small business, which is the engine of employment.

❧

A sturdy, well-rooted bureaucracy can resist dynamite.

❧

Government will usually spend more than it collects in taxes, so raising taxes may not by itself balance the budget. Increasing growth is more promising.

Tyranny

Tyrants are sometimes small men from the periphery: Attila, a dwarf from Central Asia; Napoleon from Corsica; Stalin from Georgia; Hitler from Austria.

❧

Supreme power will find a legal justification for breaking its promise.

❧

For private corruption, which can be overcome, tyranny substitutes state corruption, from which there is no escape.

Put Not Your Trust in Princes

says the Good Book. But who are these princes? Since it helps to use the right names for things, here are some categories:

A real prince or king, a ruler. This includes a tyrant called "president" who rules a "republic" — Syria, Haiti or North Korea — but is in fact a hereditary monarch. The Pope is a non-hereditary monarch. (His title of Pontifex Maximus or "Chief Bridgebuilder" — over the Tiber — came from the Roman religion.)

❧

A nominal king. Most kings, e.g., of Sweden or Britain, have only a ceremonial role, and their countries, in spite of retaining some of the paraphernalia of royalty, are not kingdoms but republics. These countries do have legally valid but powerless nobilities, including princes.

❧

Both China, which calls itself a republic, and Saudi Arabia, which calls itself a kingdom (and has thousands of princes) are oligarchies.

❧

There are also descendants of formerly titled persons whose countries have abolished those ranks, often long, long, ago. Some of these are formerly authentic, but even then empty titles. The present Republic of Georgia, for instance, at one time bestowed the title of "prince" (*knej*) on substantial farmers. French or Italian aristocratic titles that have been defunct for centuries are still asserted, even though there is no chance whatsoever of reinstatement.

❧

The heir of a ruler—the pretender—of a former kingdom that is now a republic, does have a certain status, since there may be a wild chance of a restoration.

⅔

If a princely family is very old and very grand it has standing even in the absence of a country—e.g., the Habsburgs. (The Liechtensteins point out that they gave their family name to the country, not vice versa.)

⅔

Bogus titles. Austrians, Italians and others who had an ancestor with a title are prone to call themselves by that title, and display a coat of arms, although they are younger sons of younger sons of younger sons, or even daughters or more remote kin. You can buy an English "incorporeal hereditament" called "lord of the manor" for several thousand pounds that does *not* entitle you to call yourself "Lord," which a few people have been known to do. (Entirely bogus orders, like the many fake knights of Malta, are a rich subject.) Some Europeans assume extinct titles by an adoption process or by acquiring a piece of land, an absurd pretension.

⅔

So anyway, in what princes should we not put our trust? Answer: The real ones, category one. (And perhaps, for different reasons, the completely fake ones, category seven.)

Democracy

Freedom of thought is a precondition of economic development, which is a precondition of political freedom. Thought control strangles the Arab world. However, democracy brings inflation.

⅔

Like freedom, democracy is won in stages, not created. It requires a free press, an independent judiciary, independent trade unions, an army obedient to civilian authority, a network of associations, and a middle class strong enough to resist the encroachments of government. These require a long time and an educated population.

⅔

There can be no liberty without private property, since without property the citizen is a ward of the state. (One of Bismarck's big ideas was to control the population through state pensions.) However, since the state protects property, it has some claim on it, and should tax enormous inheritances.

A State Is Heartless

The *raison d'état* will always prevail over conscience.

Fiat justitia ruat coelum, said Kant, that difficult but fascinating philosopher: "Let justice be done though the heavens fall." But narrow virtue can be disastrous in large matters.

❧

Communism, Circling from the Left, Merges with Fascism Circling from the Right

❧

Great Matters Are Small Ones Writ Large

Wars resemble family squabbles or even dogfights. Galaxies look like magnified pond water.

❧

To Achieve, Be Willing to Let Others Take the Credit

❧

Those You Don't Consult Will Oppose Your Plan

❧

A Politician Is Always There When He Needs You

❧

WEALTH

Money Is a Fungible Unit of Power

That is, the units are identical and can be substituted freely. A warlord, a tycoon, the Pope, and a movie starlet all have different kinds of power, which can be equated through money. Comrade Mao said that power grows out of the barrel of a gun, and with a gun you can indeed rob a bank or take over a province. But with money you can hire an army, buy the starlet's favors, or influence Vatican arrangements. The Medici's grip on power was based on controlling the taxes.

The True Tax Rate Is Never Calculated Correctly

For an American, it includes federal, state and municipal income taxes, property taxes, estate taxes, and sales taxes. Also, one's pro-rata share of corporate taxes already paid on dividends. Then, one should adjust further for the rigor with which the taxes on the books are actually collected. And for some city-dwellers, the tax penalty should include the pretax cost of children's private schooling of a quality that Europeans take for granted. (Public schools on the Continent are better than American private schools.) If a private school costs $35,000 a year, or $50,000 before tax, and lasts for 15 years, then you have several million dollars per family that American professionals pay and their European counterparts do not.

A Family Business Fortifies Family Spirit

When the McBurp Plumbing Supply Company is sold and transformed into an elegant trust fund, the grandchildren prefer to think of themselves as perfumed dilettanti, whose role in life is to spend gracefully. So be slow to sell a family firm: The moral cost may be high.

The Rich Should Remain Immersed in Everyday Life

Walled chateaux and limousines with dark windows are partial death. Isolated from the gritty stimuli of the everyday world we lose our capacities, like cave fish. Similarly, when a fortune is large enough so that the cost of things means nothing, one loses the sweet attachments that bind us to home and community.

The Very Rich Worry Ceaselessly About Money

They must, to become rich. Then the habit persists. Working like a fiend to become enormously rich is like body-building until you become the size of a bear, then a moose, then an elephant: only attractive to other compulsives. And after that, your booty risks corrupting your children.

※

It is not always worthwhile to work like a demon to get rich, and then work hard to give the money away again, sometimes doing more harm than good. Often it would have been better to leave it where it was.

※

J. J. Forrester (1801–1862) had enjoyed a fine career in the Portuguese wine trade. His boat with lady guests capsized at Cachao de Valeira, where he was dragged to the bottom by his moneybelt. (The ladies, buoyed by their crinolines, remained afloat.)

Inflation

The dollar has lost nine-tenths of its value in the last fifty years.

PHILOSOPHY

A Great Issue Is Never Resolved

It drifts from the front page of the newspaper to the middle, to the back, and finally right out of the paper, still unresolved.

Of Ultimate Causes, Little Is Knowable

We assign words and equations, but at the end lies mystery.

Our World

Is it a gift from our forebears, or a loan from our children?

❧

The Wonder of the Natural World Passes All Imagining at All Levels: Quasars, Pheromones, Viruses

❧

"Those Who Cannot Remember the Past Are Condemned to Repeat It"

Yes, but also those who *do* remember: They are dragged along by the *Zeitgeist*. For that matter, those who cannot remember the past *lose* their past. Strange that the great Santayana himself is now remembered only for that line. And astonishing that entire civilizations, with their languages, their messiahs, their wars, their Homers, Shakespeares, and Aristotles, are irretrievably lost.

Times Change, But Rules Remain

Circumstances create customs, which crystallize into laws, even religions. Then the circumstances change, while the rules survive.

The prejudices of our youth ossify as "common sense." Later facts require breaking the old bones and building new ones . . . a process too painful for most.

The Future

The seeds of future events lie under our feet, right now, but are inordinately difficult to collect, weigh and evaluate.

≈

The suspect fraternity of fortunetellers includes economists.

≈

Not only is the future unpredictable, but also how in the future people will view the past, including us.

Two, Three, Many Cultures

C. P. Snow refers to the "two cultures": the scientists, unaware of the sonnets of Shakespeare,* and the humanists, ignorant of the Second Law of Thermodynamics, but there are many more. Spiritual growth;** government (including law and military matters); literature; music; the fine arts and the decorative arts; humankind (including sociology, anthropology, philosophy, medicine and psychology); physical development, including yoga and sport; the machinery of living (entertaining, cooking, furniture, clothes); business (including manufacturing, services and finance). All of these cultures have their own traditions, schools, literature, libraries, and to each of them many devote all their lives, indifferent to the other categories.

*T. J. Hogg describes a Cambridge mathematician who was persuaded to read *Paradise Lost*. "What does it prove?" he said, "There is more instruction in half a page of Euclid! A man might read Milton's poem a hundred, or a thousand times, and he would never learn that the angles at the base of an isosceles triangles are equal!"

**Tolstoy: "Our work at the improvement of our soul is the most important work in the world."

Living

Do not fret about the "purpose" of life. That idea is a human construction.

Duty

People in a great position — rulers, military commanders and heads of major enterprises — must accept the path of duty rather than pleasure. The rest of us should settle for contentment, since protracted unhappiness degrades the immune system, so you become sick, and a bother to everybody.

ॐ

The Measure of Your Life Is How You Play the Cards You Are Dealt

ॐ

Savor the Texture of Your Life

Indeed, rejoice in the beauty and poetry of everyday life.

War and Peace

For the Greeks, war, the natural condition of mankind, engendered heroic deeds that would resound forever. For us, glory is a bubble, so we shun conflict.

Popular Success Vulgarizes What It Touches

Hope instead for the esteem of noble minds.

History

Usually, it seems inevitable that history would evolve as it did, even though many decisive battles, such as Waterloo and Gettysburg, could easily have gone the other way.

Vast Ideas Breed Misery

And often do more harm than good. So the prudent are skeptics. Keynes marveled at practical businessmen becoming slaves to the ideas of defunct economists, whereupon he himself became such a cult figure.

The Opiate

Politics, not, as claimed by Marx, religion, is the opiate of the masses.

ᢓᢏ

A revolution is sometimes necessary. However, its slogans, while also necessary, are false.

Book Learning Brings At Best Partial Understanding

It takes a narrow focus to do one thing well, and it does not follow that you can also do other things well. Nevertheless, specialists—writers, professors—often conclude that they possess universal wisdom.

ᢓᢏ

The real point of early education is to make the mind a powerful and flexible instrument, not just to fill it with facts, and of course to make the student a good citizen.*

ᢓᢏ

"If a man's wit be wandering, let him study the mathematics," said Bacon. However, some people are no good at math. Let them polish their brains studying what they can handle, such as law or bridge or chess; or, best of all, the classics.

ᢓᢏ

The first duty of a teacher is to impart his love of the subject.

---

*"I have no respect whatever for any study whose purpose is making money." (Seneca, *Letters of a Stoic*)

Organized Religion

Churches, in addition to their spiritual functions,* satisfy our need for ceremony.

⅋

Perhaps the paraphernalia of religion — icons, statues, saints, miracles — are aids to faith. But is that religion, or, as Islam insists, superstition?

⅋

A god is whatever people bow down to.

⅋

Some houses of worship are emptying because the faithful think that they are supposed to believe that God is a patriarch with a flowing beard peering down from 30,000 feet. But none of the Abrahamic faiths attribute to God any human attributes whatever, least of all sex. In Islam, applying any human characteristic to god is a particularly grave heresy. In all of them God created the universe in a moment of time, and is thus the algorithm behind Big Bang. Can a hydrogen explosion 13½ billion years ago be male, or "good"? All such words and images are misleading as applied to the creator.

⅋

Still less could it be predicted from the primeval chaos that particular events would come about today.

---

*"I sought for the greatness and genius of America in her commodious harbors and her ample rivers, and it was not there; in her fertile fields and boundless prairies, and it was not there; in her rich mines and her vast world of commerce, and it was not there. Not until I went to the churches of America and heard her pulpits aflame with righteousness did I understand the secret of her genius and power. America is great because she is good, and if America ever ceases to be good, America will cease to be great." (de Tocqueville)

Perversity of Gods

"The gods" seem ill disposed to prayers for specific benefits: If they are answered, expect tears.* Instead, pray for strength in adversity, charity in good fortune, and persistence in justice.

~

They also like to deflate the puffed-up and over-confident. "He thinks that, does he? He says that, does he?" WHACK!

The Greatest Teachers Usually Do Not Write, but Preach

. . . Jesus, Moses, Mohammed, Buddha, Lao-Tse, Socrates . . .

~

A Genius Is Willing to Look Foolish and Is Often Slightly Crazy
~

Our Games Reflect Our National Identities:

For the Spaniards, the tragedy of the *corrida*; for the Japanese, yielding only to strike, in judo and *go*. Forward march, bang, bang! in American football and basketball. For the Russians, the tricky combinations of chess.

~

To teach the young about life, find a game in which things reverse in mid-course, so that the leaders will be shoved back. (One such game is Chutes and Ladders.) The extreme life strategy, like over-specialization in evolution, loses out eventually to the solid, flexible middle.

Wei Wu Wei ("Act Without Acting")

Quail hunting, on which I spend some weeks a year, is an unrecognized Zen art. As in archery and swordsmanship, you must empty the mind and act instantaneously, without thought.

---

*When Laius of Thebes prayed for worthy offspring, the Oracle announced that his son would slay him.

Lowlier than Thou

A popular person tells stories against himself—to appear modest.

The Distasteful Is Renamed Frequently

The latrine has been "toilet" (from French, the "little cloth" on a bedside table), "water closet," "lavatory," "lounge," "loo," "powder room," "cloak room," "restroom" or whatever.

❧

"Frankly," "To Be Perfectly Honest": Preludes to Deception?

❧

If Everybody Knew What Others Said About Them, Nobody Would Speak to Anybody.

❧

Average

For using the word "average" without explanation, e.g. arithmetic mean, median or mode, which change the sense drastically, the punishment should be garroting.

Resignation

Since traditional agricultural societies are zero-sum systems, the population expands to the limit of the carrying capacity, after which resignation, the immemorial virtue of the peasant, is appropriate. In a modern economy impatient activity brings great benefits.

Professors

As a gynecologist need not be a woman, a professor of philosophy is rarely a Socrates.

Dreaming

Most of us are sleepwalkers, marionettes. Awake: Change and grow.

VIRTUE

Friendship

A fine rule: In their good times, my friends may not hear from me. In their bad times, always.

Charity

In dispensing charity, never take the part of the magnanimous donor. Present yourself as doing a job.

❧

"Shameful"—A Good Word

❧

Excellence

High achievement and perfection of character are rarely joined. A Washington, a Lee, Pericles or Epaminondas appears once a century.

The Truly Mortal Sin Is Pride

Repeat, "We are unprofitable servants."

Gandhi's "Seven Sins"

Wealth without work, pleasure without conscience, knowledge without character, commerce without morality, science without humanity, worship without sacrifice, and politics without principle.

❧

Perhaps better than trying to suppress people's bad side is encouraging the good side.

"Pascal's Wager"

Pascal argues that Christian doctrine may be true, so in obeying it one loses nothing, and perhaps avoids going to hell. A contemptible theory. On that reasoning one could worship Satan.

Prudence

Prudence, perhaps surprisingly, is the first of the four temporal Christian virtues.

Malice

In condemning those we do not know we describe ourselves. Our proclamations about the world and mankind reflect our own nature.

Venality Is Often Draped in Religiosity

Religious-based scams collect a billion dollars a year, not including the revenues of doubtful churches. (See *Forbes*, June 10, 2002).

One Can Live Virtuously in Any Walk of Life

Joseph, a carpenter; Peter, a fisherman; Spinoza, a lens-grinder.

❧

Perhaps wait until you are older to become respectable. While young, be free. Life tames the egotism of youth, like the rambunctiousness of a colt.

Better Hypocritical than Amoral

La Rochefoucauld is more elegant: "Hypocrisy is the homage that vice pays to virtue." Dante reserves a nice slot in hell for those who take a neutral position in moments of moral crisis. The weak shun controversy and collect jolly companions. But the virtuous can expect to be shunned, denounced, or indeed, martyred.

The Loner Makes People Uneasy

But philosophers, like compasses, must find their own direction.

Praise Good Deeds

It is niggling to complain that they are selfishly motivated. Leave motivations to God.

Examples

A good example is much more powerful than any specific result. St. Martin, remembered only for dividing his cloak with a beggar, became the most popular family name in France.*

❧

Traditional children's tales are often gruesome, but they inculcate virtue and provide consolation. Today, through a cultural Gresham's Law, the cutesy Disney stories push them aside, so that instead of learning prudence and courage, children are told to keep grinning.

❧

It is Easier to Achieve Your Objectives than to Choose Worthy Ones, or to Enjoy Them Once Achieved

❧

Acceptance

With a sigh, we resign ourselves to the misfortunes of others.

---

*The only thing known about Saint George is that he *didn't* slay the dragon, since there are no dragons. And of course Saint Nicholas, bishop of Myra, Turkey, does not fly about behind reindeer (that's Odin). Nor does he descend chimneys: Such a link between earth and a higher world is common in sacred iconography, e.g. the Tree of Life.

ART

Writing or journalism to be read today and forgotten next year is an artisanal product, like any other.

҈

Work that aims high may be *art*.

҈

Art that will be read generations hence may be *literature*.

҈

Great art enriches and ennobles life.

҈

At the summit is *magic*, enchantment.

҈

Great art is grave, simple, touching and often elegiac: "Tell them in Lacedaemon, passer-by, that here obedient to their word we lie," and "Our revels now are ended . . . ," and "*Mignonne allons voir si la rose . . .*" and "Had we but world enough and time . . ." and "The world of dew . . ."*

The Classics

The Greek and Roman classics immerse us in the great sweep of history. They reveal a noble point of view, and require the student to be accurate.**

҈

We are quite right to call various neuroses the Oedipus complex, the Electra complex, and so on. Great art reaches deep into human nature.

---

*The world of dew/ Is a world of dew. / And yet/ And yet . . . (Issa, on the death of his last child; the neighbors sought to console him with Buddhist platitudes about the fleeting reality of life.)

**Since the facts are all in, we can't impose our ideas on the material; and when translating we can't fudge, while soft studies invite wishful thinking and impressionism.

Beauty

Beauty ennobles us, and propagates itself, like a candle lighting another candle.

❧

Nourish a child's eye by surrounding him with lovely objects.

❧

Taking many photographs blunts the resonance of beauty.

❧

What does original art have that even a perfect reproduction lacks? Charisma?

Portraits

Don't wait until you're old to have your portrait painted.*

❧

Don't grin.**

Practical Viewing

To escape the crowd at an exhibition, arrive at opening time, move promptly to the far end, and then work your way back.

❧

Inspect the postcards in the museum store upon entering as a cue to the objects of greatest interest.

*Or join a club: aging, you generate adversaries.

**Sargent's sitters annoyed him by smirking, and later asking, "Isn't there something wrong with the mouth, Mr. Sargent?" He described a portrait as a picture with something wrong with the mouth.

Four Commandments of Good Prose

Write short sentences.

❧

Seek vigorous, colorful verbs.*

❧

Favor Anglo-Saxon words over Latin ones.

❧

Use the active voice, not the passive.

Style

How bitter for a great artist to be at odds with the esthetic canon of his time! Once it was imposed religion or morals. Today it is the need to be novel, which kills elegance and lucidity. Novelty should flow from inner power, not be an objective. And political correctness, a disaster!

❧

The English feel that good form in a writer, as in a man of the world, includes being witty. Wit being cultured and aristocratic, Americans distrust it, particularly in politicians.

❧

Shun the merely clever.

❧

Often what separates first-rate art from merely good art is the point of view. One thinks of Thornton Wilder,** a marvelous stylist, whose work, like Hemingway's, is flawed by sentimentality; or Swinburne, a lord of language with little to say. A discouraging combination is perfect technique coupled with sick taste, like Dali.

---

*The verbs *propel* the sentence. Write, "The statue *stands* in the square," not "The statue *is* in the square."

**His wonderful close to *The Bridge of San Luis Rey* is rightly famous: "There is a land of the living and a land of the dead and the bridge is love. . . ." Actually, though, love binds the living to each other, and the bridge to the past is art.

If the New York School Are Real Poets, My Parrot Is Caruso

Alas, most of today's poets display neither style, nor the ability to touch the heart, or to be memorable. We cannot live without poetry, but in our time the poetic river has dried up and gone underground. It reappears in the lyrics of popular music: trashy, but still poetry. Most Americans cannot recite a line by a living poet (probably the first time in history of which this is true), while the young, plugged into CD players, absorb endless pop lyrics, and their elders delight in the lyrics of *My Fair Lady*.

Hispanic Countries Remain Obsessed with Their Traditional Music

Portugal and the haunting fire of the fado; Spain and the flamenco; Argentina, the tango; Brazil, the samba.

Missing Words

Thought is constrained by available words. Our culture leans to the strong words at the extremity of the scale: hot-cold, black-white, good-bad. The middle words—tepid, gray—are weak. We do not even have a word for morally neutral. And yet nothing is absolutely hot, cold, good or bad.

English lacks a word for an infant's desperate need for love, perhaps the strongest emotion; or a grandmother's craving to care for the children; or for our fellow in-laws,* or for the virtue of steadfast resistance to evil,** or for the joy of finding a lost passport or address book,*** or for satisfaction at the ills of others,**** or for smarmy, fake moralizing.*****

---

*In Spanish, *consuegros*; Italian, *consuoceri*; Greek, *symbethera*; Yiddish, *machintenster*.

**In German, *Zivilcourage*. "Civil courage" is needed in English.

***I offer *Wiedergefundenfreude*.

****In German, *Schadenfreude*. (In reverse, *tristitia de bonis alienis* is annoyance at the good fortune of others).

*****Poshlost* in Russian.

54

Literary Quarrels Can Be Astonishingly Envenomed

How Do I Write a Book?

If you have to ask, don't. Creation, like love, is a compulsion, from which the craft will follow.

❧

First live, then write.

❧

In plotting a novel, keep the hero in trouble.

❧

Carry a card or notebook to record your ideas immediately.

Columns

Start with a "grabber," e.g., a little story.

❧

A good column leans against the wind, and proves its point, and contains one new fact.

❧

Writing a regular column sucks up all your thoughts, like the ventilator in a hotel kitchen.

Translation

As an iridescent fish is lifted from the river, its luster fades. So with poetry in translation.

"Financial Journalism Is a Branch of the Entertainment Business"

. . . said Jim Michaels, my wonderful *Forbes* editor. Indeed, so is most journalism. To support the ads, newspapers want *stories*, not studies.

❧

People will pay for predictions about the unknowable, including astrology and macroeconomics. Also for lies, including pseudo-science myths like pyramid power, alien abductions, or diets of the month.

❧

Journalists scare the reader while blaming someone they don't like.

INVESTING

There is Nothing in the World Like Compound Interest

Specifically, $2,000 invested in each of your first eight working years can become $1 million by age 65.

❧

Give children highly appreciated securities, rather than cash. More important than the tax advantage is revealing the power of long-term compounding.

Real Investing

Only buy a stock that you'd be glad to hold in the absence of any market, like a house.

❧

Investment Opportunity Consists of the Difference Between the Perception and the Reality

❧

Investment and Temperament

Choose the investing technique that corresponds to your temperament—growth, bargain-hunting, real estate, science, absolute return, or whatever—and stick to it for a long time. You will not do better by hopping about. Mastering a new investing style is the greatest trick of all, but is utterly counterintuitive, and most people shouldn't try. Still, if you can manage it, an excellent way to invest is to buy the best fund in an unpopular strategy. Start small, and follow up if the strategy starts to work. But when that strategy has been successful for some years, prepare to move on.

Look Up What the Great Investors Are Buying, and Select from Their Picks

Also, follow insider buying of a stock you find interesting. Insiders sell for many reasons, but they only buy for one: to make money.

Train's Fourth Law: Nothing Exceeds Like Success

Beware of an investment idea—particularly a true idea that is universally accepted: It will suffer the worst decline. The words "XYZ can only go up" are a fire bell for the experienced investor. If all the kids get on the south end of the seesaw because that's the end that's going up, it can't go up.

The Time of Deepest Gloom

Do some buying when times are desperate.* Markets exaggerate, so if fair value might be between fifteen and thirty, the market price might gyrate between ten and fifty.

❧

The stock market offers a marvelous lab for psychology. The wiggly line of the Dow Jones average is an encephalogram of the human race.

Buying Art

Only buy what you love and understand.

❧

When a country gets rich, it buys back its heritage: American antiques after World War II, then Japanese sword furniture, then Middle Eastern antiquities, then Fabergé and the Russians, the Chinese, and so on.

❧

Buy a craft that is being re-rated as art: American folk painting, African artifacts, Japanese "floating world" prints, photographs.

---

*The dictum, "Buy when there's blood in the streets," attributed to a "Baron Rothschild" (of whom there have been dozens) is quite true, particularly of war scares. But don't try to catch the dead low. Anywhere in the bottom area is fine.

The Art of the Specific

To invest successfully, one does not need to know a lot, only a few things that are both *true* and *original*. You should know more than other people about something particular. Trying to know a great many things superficially is useless, since others will know more about each, and the process takes time. Buying what others already believe in means overpaying.

Selling

Selling just because a stock goes down is utterly amateurish, as though when you bought a picture you offered to sell it again if a *lower* offer was received.

Avoid IPOs

The business of the underwriter is to assure that initial public offerings are overpriced. They usually decline in due course. Particularly, avoid them at times when most are going to an immediate premium.

Cycles

Not only the whole market but each asset class separately moves in a typical cyclical pattern, based not on reason but emotion. Buying puts prices up, attracting more buying, until the process collapses, like a waterspout; then the process operates in reverse.

A Chinese Maxim

Cross the river, groping for the stones. (That is, start out buying a small amount of a stock and see how things progress.)*

Don't Sell All *of a Great Growth Stock*

It may seem too high, but there may be merits you don't know. In theory you can sell out and buy back cheaper. In practice, you don't.

---

*Another one, unrelated, is, "Kill the chicken to frighten the monkey." (By a minor act of great severity, signal your menace to a dangerous potential malefactor.)

Great Companies

The pearl of great price in a company is a drive to innovate.

⁊₭

Things are always changing, so a great company, in a time of change, must be highly flexible.

⁊₭

A great company has a continuing program of cost-cutting.

⁊₭

A great company should have an outstanding leader. (See page 24).

⁊₭

At the top, outstanding business skill is much more important than technical skill.

Analyzing

You must understand the *culture* of a company, which is often transmitted by stories. Ask for some about the leader. (As a director, Warren Buffett tolerated the notoriously rotten "Liar's Poker" culture of Salomon Brothers, which then blew apart, giving him a ghastly time.)

⁊₭

Earnings can be manipulated. Free cash flow and return on equity are more reliable.

⁊₭

You needn't visit a company you want to invest in, but can talk to its customers, competitors and suppliers. Learn about a car and its maker from the repair mechanic, not the showroom salesman.

⁊₭

"By the time the smoke has lifted, the train has left the station." (When you have enough information, act. Do not write a thesis.)

⁊₭

Five years is a good investment perspective.

⁊₭

The language of business is figures, as that of music is notes. So if you can't understand accounting, don't invest for yourself.

❧

Ignore tips, which are usually duds and often self-interested.

Advising

Intellectual honesty and industriousness will hold most clients in a professional organization.

❧

Be the first to tell the client bad news.

❧

Admit what you don't know, and then find it out.

❧

It's easier to find a company that will stay great than an investment manager who will stay great. A company is a whole system, while an outstanding investment manager usually depends on one man, subject to burnout.

Bull and Bear

In a bear market, the public believes that the world is ending; in a bull market, that the trees will grow up to the sky. Neither is likely.

❧

There's no one as bearish as a sold-out bull.

❧

The public measures a bull market up from the bottom, and a bear market down from the top. Logically, though, one should think of each as half of a cycle that started in the middle of the previous phase.

❧

Stocks seem wildly expensive all the way up in a bull market, and crazily cheap all the way down in a bear market.

❧

The market is like a love affair: In the exalté phase everything is forgiven. Going down, nothing.

Train's Fifth Law

The end of every bull market blowout is that time's variation of a margin account; enough different from the last time so that it isn't recognized. LBOs, Chinese paper, junk bonds, unhedged hedge funds, mortgage "structured finance," derivatives. . . .

Buying

In your travels, collect only prime objects — presumably antique.
A tribal object that has actually been used for the intended purpose is greatly preferable to one made for sale.

⁂

The price of wine increases twice as fast as its quality: thus, a $20 bottle is only 50% better than a $10 bottle, a $40 bottle 50% better than a $20 bottle, and so on.

⁂

The "house wine" in a restaurant is usually overpriced. (But a restaurant that is somewhat too costly for the quality of its food will be more attentive and less crowded.) The cheapest wine on the list in an excellent restaurant can be interesting, since a very good restaurant won't sell any bad wine.

⁂

Hardcover books, if the type is more legible, can be a better buy, particularly secondhand, than paperbacks.

⁂

Deal with a vendor whose reputation is tied to that particular service. E.g., do not buy a tie in a museum store: The knot becomes tiny.

⁂

Bargains are found in an antique store where objects are piled on one another.

⁂

Resist buying clothes on sale that aren't exactly what you want.

Business Dealings with Amateurs Invite Imbroglios

In Business, Find out the Reputation of Those You are Dealing with

Do they follow the spirit of an agreement, regardless of the documents?

Is their attitude, "I never break a contract unless I have to"—including the disgusting excuse, "My lawyer tells me . . ."?

Do they calculate what it will cost you in legal fees and trouble to enforce an agreement?

People in business are aware of these attitudes, but for the civilized person they come as a shock.

Trading—Commodities, Derivatives, or Stocks— Is a Hopeless Casino

The immensely rich Fribourg family owned Continental Grain, one of the three largest commodity dealers in the world. It created a subsidiary, Conti-Commodity, to make the joys of commodity trading available to a broad public. ContiCommodity launched two commodity trading mutual funds. Both went bust. Then ContiCommodity went bust. The remainder was traded to Refco, a giant commodities trading firm. Then Refco went bust.

Wall Street's Attitude: "When the Ducks Quack, Feed 'Em."

That's the brokers' attitude toward suckers in the latter stages of a bull market. Thus, the "seminars" conducted on commodity speculation are vicious, and the ease of day trading on the Internet impoverishes many. A few people will become addicted to gambling, and court ruin.

The Warning

Wall Street likes to say that the market has anticipated five of the last three recessions. That's because a market drop, like a masthead lookout calling out that there are rocks ahead, warns the helmsman to change course.

Beware the Icarus Syndrome

Hot managers, like conquerors, burn out. Arrogance, too-rapid growth and the resulting complexity; age, and loss of concentration do it. The hot manager carries much more baggage down with him than when he started up, and often loses more money for his investors as a class than he ever made for them.

Investment Performance Is Not Investor Performance

The average investor in a good fund only does about half as well as the fund as a whole. The reason is that most fund shareholders tend to buy near tops and after four or five years sell near bottoms.

Train's Third Law: "Most Things Don't Work"

An inexperienced investor will probably lose money in a new venture.* The good deals are shown first to the professionals, who can decide crisply. In a startup, the investors put up all the money for about two-thirds of a company with uncertain prospects and experimental management. By waiting a few years for a market washout, you can buy a great company for less than its working capital, with skilled management in place, and the other assets, including the excellent business itself, free.

---

*"A fool and his money are welcome everywhere," observes Warren Buffett.

Strategy

"Don't swing for the fences. Steady gains will get you where you want to go."*

And indeed, here's a bit more: "Understand the [investment] process, the way you should understand medicine and government but don't try too hard yourself. In pursuing great wealth you become a money-person. You see the world through dollar-sign binoculars.

"Then, the exaggeration of any principle becomes its undoing, as the excess of a stimulant becomes a poison, and changing greed from a sin into a commandment dissolves the soul of a family. The children of excessive privilege are often purposeless and unhappy. What gain is worth that loss?

"Indeed, the hurly-burly of humanity, from which great wealth insulates itself, its joys and trials, is what we're made for.

"The rational approach is to trust in a sufficiency of wealth as a by-product of a useful life. Happy are those who find fulfillment in their families, their work, and their civic duties, and hope for the best."

*This, from one of my books, was rather surprisingly cited by Andrew Tobias in *Parade* as the most useful advice by a living investment guru. So here it is again.

LOVE

The Risk

The great joy of life is to love and be loved. That means you must give yourself away completely, accepting the risk of suffering.

The Addiction

Chemically speaking, passionate love is an addiction, like others, so breaking off can be excruciatingly painful.

Roles

Wives are young men's mistresses, companions for middle age, and old men's nurses.

— Francis Bacon

Bertrand Russell

I have never imagined such love. I have had the feeling too that I ought to keep it back from you so as not to interfere with your freedom — but I can't. . . . With you there is life and joy and peace and all good things — away from you there is turmoil and anguish and blank despair.

— Letter to Lady Ottoline Morrell*

*One of two thousand.

Men and Women

"Man's love is of man's life a thing apart. It is woman's whole existence."
— Lord Byron

Soldier's Homecoming

"First I took off my boots, then I laid my wife, then I took off my pack."*
— Traditional account, in all armies

Arrangement

A canny matchmaker, such as an experienced, wise aunt, can sometimes hatch a union that will last into old age, after youthful passions have faded.** The Chinese say that you can put a cold pot on a cold stove, and it will cool off. Put a cold pot on a hot stove and it will warm up and stay hot.

The Long Term

For long-term happiness marry your best friend: a spouse always cheerful and intelligent, never grappling for moral superiority. A good test is that the two just babble a lot with each other.

De Profundis

Dear Alf, I seen you last night in my dream. O my dear I cried at waking up. What a silly girl you been and got. The pain is bad this morning but I laugh at the sollum clocks of the sisters and the sawbones. I can see they

---

*While Marlborough, returning from the wars, with soldierly dispatch "pleasured me in his boots," according to his wife. (Commanders don't carry packs.)

**The Japanese see in cherry blossoms a symbol of young love, being all too brief.

think I am booked but they don't know what has befalen between you and me. How could I die and leave you Dear. I spill my medicin this morning thinking of my Dear. Hopeing this finds you well no more now from yours truly Liz.

— Cited in Love, by Walter de la Mare
The writer died a few days later.

Ama et quod vis fac

Love and do what you will.

— St. Augustine

Power

Love dispels fear.*

*Cf. 1 John 4:18.

ACKNOWLEDGEMENTS

I am grateful to friends who have looked over the text and suggested
useful cuts, particularly Linda Kelly, Nina Train Choa,
Sara Perkins, Nina Lobanov-Rostovsky,
and Kenneth Lubbock.

copyright © 2011 John Train

ISBN 978-1-1658-319-4

available from artisan@midcoast.com